FRANCHISING IN CAPE VERDE 2014

Legal and Business Considerations

KENDAL H. TYRE, JR., EXECUTIVE EDITOR
DIANA VILMENAY-HAMMOND, MANAGING EDITOR
COURTNEY L. LINDSAY, II, ASSISTANT EDITOR

LEXNOIR FOUNDATION

FOURTH QUARTER 2013

LexNoir Foundation is the charitable, educational arm of LexNoir, an international network of lawyers connecting the African Diaspora.

This publication, *Franchising in Cape Verde 2014: Legal and Business Considerations*, contains excerpts from *Franchising in Africa 2014: Legal and Business Considerations*. Both works are published by LexNoir Foundation and reflect the points of view of the authors and editors as of the date of publication and do not necessarily represent the opinions, interpretations, or positions of the law firms or organizations with which they are affiliated, nor the opinions, interpretations or positions of LexNoir Foundation or LexNoir.

www.lexnoir.org

Table of Contents

About the Editors and Authors iv

About the Book viii

Franchising in Cape Verde

João Afonso Fialho
Miranda Correia Amendoeira & Associados

I. Introduction 1

- A. Historical Background of Country 1
- B. Economy of the Country 1
- C. Franchise Legal Overview 2

II. Regulatory Requirements 2

- A. Pre-Sale Disclosure 2
- B. Governmental Approvals, Registrations, Filing Requirements 3
- C. Limits of Fees and Typical Term of Franchise Agreement 3

III. Currency 3

IV. Taxes, Tariffs, and Duties 4

- A. Applicable Rate 4
- B. Gross-up Clauses 5

V. Trademarks 6

VI. Restrictions on Transfer 6

VII. Termination 8

VIII. Governing Law, Jurisdiction, and Dispute Resolution 8

- A. Choice of Law of Foreign Jurisdiction 8
- B. International Arbitration Dispute Resolution 10

IX. Non-Competition Provisions 11

X. Language Requirements 12

XI. Other Significant Matters 13

Bibliography of International Franchise Resources

Kendal H. Tyre, Jr., Diana Vilmenay-Hammond, Pierce Haesung Han, Courtney L. Lindsay, II and Keri McWilliams
Nixon Peabody LLP

I. General International Resources 15

II. African Resources 18

- A. Angola 19
- B. Botswana 20
- C. Cape Verde 20
- D. Egypt 20
- E. Ethiopia 20
- F. Ghana 20
- G. Libya 21
- H. Mozambique 21
- I. Nigeria 21
- J. South Africa 21
- K. Tunisia 22
- L. Zambia 22

Acknowledgment

This book could not have been written without the hard work and dedication of each of the contributing authors and editors. Thank you.

We would like to acknowledge and extend our heartfelt gratitude to Michael Collier and Maria Stallings of the Washington, D.C. office of Nixon Peabody LLP for their invaluable assistance in revising, proofing, and editing this publication.

About the Editors and Authors

Kendal H. Tyre, Jr. – Kendal is a partner in the Washington, D.C. office of Nixon Peabody LLP. He handles domestic and cross-border transactions, including mergers and acquisitions, joint ventures, strategic alliances, licensing, and franchise matters.

In his franchise and licensing practice, Kendal counsels domestic and international franchisors, franchisees, licensors, licensees and distributors regarding U.S. state and federal franchise laws as well as foreign franchise legislation in a variety of jurisdictions. Kendal drafts and provides advice with regard to franchise and license agreements, disclosure documents and area development agreements and has extensive experience drafting and negotiating a variety of other commercial agreements. His client base spans the United States and foreign countries, including South Africa, Kenya, and the United Kingdom.

Kendal is a frequent contributor to franchise publications and a frequent speaker at franchise programs held by the American Bar Association Forum on Franchising and the International Franchise Association.

Kendal is co-chair of the firm's Diversity Action Committee and its Africa Group. Kendal is also the executive director of LexNoir Foundation.

E-mail address: ktyre@nixonpeabody.com

Diana Vilmenay-Hammond – Diana is an attorney in the Washington, D.C. office of Nixon Peabody LLP. She is a member of the firm's Franchise & Distribution Team.

In her franchise practice, Diana works with domestic and international franchisors on transactional and litigation matters. Specifically, she counsels franchisor clients regarding state and federal franchise laws, disclosure and registration obligations.

Diana drafts and negotiates various commercial agreements, including international franchise and development agreements.

Diana has co-authored numerous articles on franchising and frequently co-hosted the Nixon Peabody franchise law webinar series. Topics have included:

- "Franchise Case Law Round-Up: Implications for Your Franchise," February 15, 2012;
- "Social Media Part II: Best Practices in Protecting Your Brand in the New Media," September 14, 2010; and
- "The Awuah Case: Bellwether or Outlier," May 11, 2010

Diana received her J.D. from Howard University School of Law and her B.A. from Georgetown University. She is a member of the American Bar Association (Forum on Franchising).

Email address: dvilmenay@nixonpeabody.com

Pierce Haesung Han – Pierce is an associate in Nixon Peabody's Global Business & Transactions Group. Pierce focuses his practice on three main areas, assisting clients with a variety of complex business transactions.

- Mergers & Acquisitions: Providing assistance to both public and private clients with various mergers and acquisitions, performing due diligence, drafting and negotiating transaction documents, and facilitating closing and post-closing mechanics.
- International Commercial Transactions: Drafting and negotiating a variety of commercial agreements, including international franchise and development agreements, license agreements, and purchase and sale agreements.
- Federal Securities Law Matters: Assisting public and private clients regarding federal securities laws and stock exchange rules relating to corporate governance and disclosure.

Pierce serves as the Secretary of the Asian Pacific Bar Association Educational Fund (an affiliate of the Asian Pacific American Bar Association of the Greater Washington, D.C. Area).

Pierce received his J.D. from Georgetown University Law Center and his B.A. from Case Western Reserve University. He is admitted to practice in the State of New York and the District of Columbia.

E-mail address: phan@nixonpeabody.com

Courtney L. Lindsay II – Courtney is an associate in Nixon Peabody's Corporate and Finance practice. In his corporate practice, Courtney assists for-profit and non-profit entities with transactional matters and corporate governance. In various capacities, Courtney has been involved in multiple merger and acquisition transactions, including drafting and managing due diligence.

Previously, Courtney worked in the legal and business affairs department at a national cable network, where he handled matters related to the network's LLC agreement, including drafting board and member consent agreements.

Courtney received his J.D. from the University of Virginia School of Law and his B.A. from the University of Virginia. He is admitted to practice in the Commonwealth of Virginia and the District of Columbia.

E-mail address: clindsay@nixonpeabody.com

Keri McWilliams – Keri is an associate in the Franchise & Distribution team of Nixon Peabody LLP. Keri works with clients on a number of franchising issues, including obtaining and maintaining franchise registrations in various states, responding to state inquiries regarding trade practices, ongoing compliance with state and federal regulations, and updating franchise disclosure documents. She also handles franchise sales counseling and franchise system issues.

Keri is a member of the American Bar Association's Forum on Franchising, and the Federal and Minnesota State bar associations. She is also a member of Minnesota Women Lawyers and the Minnesota Association of Black Lawyers, and a volunteer in the Volunteer Lawyers Network.

Keri received her J.D. from the Georgetown University Law Center and her B.F.A. from Washington University. She is admitted to practice in the District of Columbia and Minnesota.

E-mail address: kmcwilliams@nixonpeabody.com

João Afonso Fialho – João is a partner at Miranda Correia Amendoeira & Associados in Lisbon, Portugal, and has an extensive practice in Lusophone and Francophone African countries. He started his career in the law office of Tomás Andrade Rocha where his practice was mostly focused on litigation. In his early years of practice, João acted for a variety of clients in the finance sector, including banks, consumer credit companies, aviation companies, oil firms and automakers. From 1992 to 1997, João was also legal advisor to the Loures and the Lisbon City Halls, having participated in several projects related to the Lisbon 94-European Culture Capital initiative.

After joining Miranda Correia Amendoeira & Associados, João expended his practice considerably. In addition to a litigation practice, he became involved in several large investment projects in Portugal, Angola, Cape Verde and other jurisdictions, in such diverse areas as oil & gas, diamonds and mining, infrastructures, distribution and franchising, real estate, shipping, and aviation. João is a regular contributor to various legal publications. He was ranked as an Expert in Dispute Resolution in the 2008 to 2013 editions of the European Legal Experts Guide. João is fluent in English.

E-mail address: Joao.Fialho@mirandalawfirm.com

About the Book

Franchising in Cape Verde 2014: Legal and Business Considerations contains excerpts from the larger work, *Franchising in Africa 2014: Legal and Business Considerations*. Both books serve as practical, succinct, easy-to-use reference tools for lawyers, business people and academics to use in navigating the myriad laws and business issues impacting franchise arrangements on the African continent.

This book provides an overview of the franchise industry in Cape Verde and addresses the typical legal issues confronted when expanding a franchise system in Cape Verde. The larger work, *Franchising in Africa 2014: Legal and Business Considerations*, covers those laws governing franchising in fifteen other African countries – Angola, Botswana, Burundi, Democratic Republic of Congo, Egypt, Ethiopia, Ghana, Kenya, Mozambique, Nigeria, Rwanda, South Africa, Tunisia, Zambia and Zimbabwe.

In both books, an author, who is a legal expert in the designated jurisdiction, addresses the basic questions that a franchise lawyer would need to know to competently represent a client in expanding their franchise system to that country.

Each country chapter organizes a discussion of that country's laws under various headings and in a uniform format. Topics were sent to each country's author in the form of a questionnaire, and each author drafted responses to the questions presented. A general overview relating to the political and economic history of the country at the beginning of each chapter provides an initial context for the regulatory framework. [1]

---

1 The source of information for these sections is the Central Intelligence Agency, https://www.cia.gov/library/publications/the-world-factbook/ (last visited November 3, 2013).

Apart from an overview of the legal framework for franchising, each book contains other articles and resources that should prove useful to those in the franchise industry.

The authors for each chapter are listed at the beginning of a chapter and their biographical information is listed in the previous section, *About the Editors and Authors*.

Readers should always consult with local counsel in the relevant jurisdiction instead of relying solely on the information contained in this book. The laws governing franchising are evolving and local counsel in Cape Verde are best positioned to provide timely, relevant advice applying the current law to the particular facts of a case.

Franchising in Cape Verde

João Afonso Fialho

Miranda Correia Amendoeira & Associados

Lisbon, Portugal

Cape Verde

I. Introduction

A. Historical Background of Country

Following independence in 1975, and a tentative interest in unification with Guinea-Bissau, a one-party system was established and maintained until multi-party elections were held in 1990. Cape Verde continues to exhibit one of Africa's most stable democratic governments. Repeated droughts during the second half of the 20th century caused significant hardship and prompted heavy emigration. As a result, Cape Verde's expatriate population is greater than its domestic one.

B. Economy of the Country

This island economy suffers from a poor natural resource base, including serious water shortages exacerbated by cycles of long-term drought. The economy is service-oriented with commerce, transport, tourism, and public services accounting for about three-fourths of GDP. Although nearly 70% of the population lives in rural areas, the share of food production in GDP is low. About 82% of food must be imported. The fishing potential, mostly lobster and tuna, is not fully exploited. Cape Verde annually runs a high trade deficit financed by foreign aid and remittances from emigrants; remittances supplement GDP by more than 20%. Economic reforms are aimed at developing the private sector and attracting foreign investment to diversify the economy. Future prospects depend heavily on the maintenance of aid flows, the encouragement of tourism, remittances, and the momentum of the government's development program. Cape Verde became a member of the WTO in July 2008.

C. Franchise Legal Overview

Cape Verde has a civil law legal system. Most of the provisions governing contracts are established in the Civil Code or in other statutes.

Cape Verde

Cape Verdean contract law is governed by the principle of contractual freedom. Within the limits set forth in the law, parties may freely agree on the terms of a contract. This principle is expressly contained in the Civil Code, approved by *Decree-law 47344, of November 25, 1966*, as amended ("Civil Code").

In relation to the franchise agreements, there is no specific statute governing franchising in Cape Verde. Thus, the contractual relationship (rights and obligations) established between the parties in a franchise agreement must be construed in accordance with the provisions of the Civil Code or other statutes which may also be applicable.

In the absence of a specific statute, a franchise agreement is simply an agreement aimed at governing a relationship between two business parties, and therefore qualifies as a non-standard commercial agreement. The legal regime for this type of agreement is set forth in the Commercial Code, approved by *Letter of Law dated June 28, 1888*, as amended ("Commercial Code").

II. Regulatory Requirements

A. Pre-Sale Disclosure

Please describe any pre-sale franchise disclosure or similar requirements that may apply to franchise transactions.

No pre-sale franchise disclosure or similar requirements apply to franchise transactions under the laws of Cape Verde.

B. Governmental Approvals, Registrations, Filing Requirements

Please describe any necessary government approvals, registrations, or filing requirements that may apply to franchise transactions.

Other than the registration referred to below – *see* Section III (Currency), no other government approval, registration, or filing requirements shall apply to franchise agreements.

Notwithstanding the above, a Cape Verdean franchisor or franchisee will be subject to the regular registration procedures and filing requirements required for performing business activities in Cape Verde, such as, inter alia, commercial registration with the Companies Registrar, if applicable; tax registration with the Tax Office; obtaining a commercial operations permit from the Ministry of Commerce; and an import/export license.

C. Limits of Fees and Typical Term of Franchise Agreement

Please describe any limits upon the nature and extent of fees and the term of a typical franchise agreement.

As there is no specific legal framework governing the franchise agreement, the parties are free to agree on the terms and conditions of a franchise agreement as long as they keep within certain general public policy principles established in the Constitution, the Commercial Code, and/or the Civil Code, and are in compliance with the general principles of law and justice. There are no other limits on the nature and extent of fees and the term that shall apply.

III. Currency

If all payments under a franchise agreement must be made in immediately available U.S. Dollars, please advise as to any restrictions, reporting requirements, or regulations concerning the exchange, repatriation, or remittance of U.S. Dollars.

Transfer of foreign currency into or out of Cape Verde is subject to the controls and prior authorization of the Central Bank ("*Banco de Cabo Verde*"). However, this is not a particularly restrictive regime and a relevant party is simply required to submit relevant documentation to the Central Bank prior to requesting a transfer.

In order to obtain the Central Bank's authorization, the interested party must submit a request to a commercial local bank attaching all documentation evidencing and explaining the relevant transaction. To that end, a Portuguese language translation of the agreement will most likely be necessary. The commercial bank will then liaise with the Central Bank to obtain the necessary authorization. The Bank's authorization is granted in almost all cases, particularly since there has not been an instance of a shortage of foreign currency in the last 15 years.

IV. Taxes, Tariffs, and Duties

Please do not provide any in-depth comments on tax structuring. However, please provide your general comments on the typical amount of withholding tax that would apply and whether a "gross-up" provision contained in a franchise agreement would be enforceable in your country.

A. Applicable Rate

From a Cape Verdean tax standpoint, payments as consideration for the rendering of management services, advertising, publicity, as well as royalty fees paid under a franchising agreement may trigger income tax withholding.

Cape Verde at present has only two international double taxation treaties on income tax in force, with Portugal and Macau. Apart from these treaties, there is no other available mechanism to reduce or eliminate the assessment of withholding tax in Cape Verde, thus, international tax relief for non-resident investors (besides Portuguese and Macau based investors) can only be obtained in their home jurisdiction.

Pursuant to the *Single Tax on Income Code* as approved by the *Law 127/IV/95*, of June 26, 1995 and *Decree-Law 1/96* of January 15, 1996, as amended (*Imposto Único sobre os*

Rendimentos), income, as defined in the several categories of taxable income, obtained by a non-resident franchisor from a Cape Verdean source (i.e., paid by a resident franchisee), is subject to withholding tax, depending on the nature of the payment.[2]

Given the above, according to the Cape Verde State Budget for 2010, income obtained as a consideration for the rendering of services by a non-resident franchisor is subject to a withholding of 20% of the gross income.

The term royalties, as defined under the Single Tax on Income Code, includes payments arising from the use or the right to use industrial and commercial equipment, the granting of information concerning industrial, commercial, or scientific experience and technical assistance, and, thus, royalty fees paid under a franchising agreement to a non-resident franchisor will be subject to 15% withholding.

Payments made between Cape Verde taxpayers are not subject to income tax withholding, and will be considered as business profits subject to the annual 25% Single Tax on Income.

B. Gross-up Clauses

Tax gross-up clauses are valid and contractually binding pursuant to Cape Verdean tax law and should preclude any economic loss in the event that any tax is due to the Cape Verdean tax authorities on any payments made under a franchising agreement. Notwithstanding, such clauses, from a tax standpoint, are not binding for the tax authorities since legally it is not possible to assign responsibility for the payment of any taxes in Cape Verde.

---

2 Non-resident franchisors with no permanent establishment in Cape Verde are only subject to tax on income from Cape Verdean sources.

V. Trademarks

Please advise us as to whether there are any special requirements for granting a valid trademark license, including the use of a registered user agreement or a short trademark license agreement and any required filing of such an agreement with the trademark authorities.

Intellectual property in Cape Verde is regulated by the *Cape Verdean Industrial Property Code* (*Código de Propriedade Industrial*), as approved by the *Council of Ministers' Decree 4/2007* of August 20, 2007. This Code allows one party to license a registered trademark to a third party. Article 173 of that Code is the specific provision governing the relationship between licensee and licensor. Under this Article, the trademark owner is entitled to claim its rights as owner of the trademark against the licensee. This would apply in particular when the licensee has breached any clause or provision of the licensing agreement, particularly those that deal with its term, the distinctiveness of a trademark, the nature or quality of the goods or services for which the license was granted, or any geographic limitations to the use of the licensed trademark.

The law does not establish any particular requirement or formalities to enter into a trademark license agreement or to file the licensing agreement with the trademark office.

VI. Restrictions on Transfer

Please advise as to whether there are any restrictions (1) on a franchisor to restrict transfers by a master franchisee, any interest in a master franchisee, or the assets of the master franchisee or (2) the ability of a master franchisee to control and/or restrict transfers of a subfranchisee's rights under a master franchise agreement, interest in the subfranchisee, or the assets of the subfranchisee.

Cape Verdean law does not set forth any specific restrictions on the franchisor's ability to restrict the (i) transfers by a master franchisee, (ii) transfers of an interest in a master franchisee, or (iii) transfers of assets of the master franchisee, nor does it do so on the master's franchisee's ability to control and/or restrict (i) transfers of a subfranchisee's rights under a master franchise agreement, (ii) transfers of an interest in the subfranchisee, or (iii) transfers of assets of the subfranchisee.

Considering the private nature of a franchise agreement, the parties may, within the scope of their contractual freedom, introduce such clauses as they see fit, provided they are not unlawful or against public order.

In relation to the assignment of a party's contractual position, the Civil Code sets forth that neither party may assign its contractual position without the prior consent of the other.

In relation to the subfranchise agreement, the same principles apply. In other words, the assignment by one of the parties is subject to the consent of the other and it may also be subject to the prior consent of a third party, unless the relevant consent is previously agreed in the contract. The law allows for general, non-specific consent without the name of the assignee being set.

Under Cape Verdean law, it is permissible to subject to the consent of the franchisor the right of the franchisee's shareholders to transfer their (direct and/or indirect) interests in the share capital of the franchisee. Also, the parties may further agree that the subfranchisee's shareholders may only transfer their (direct and/or indirect) interests in the subfranchisee's share capital upon the franchisor's approval. However, in both cases, the shareholders accepting these restrictions must execute the relevant agreement.

Under the law, the parties may agree on a clause by virtue of which the franchisee/subfranchisee becomes obliged, upon termination of the franchise/subfranchise agreement, to transfer to the franchisor/franchisee (or to other entity nominated by the franchisor) all the assets used in the franchise/subfranchise. On the other hand, the same provision may be agreed between the parties, but in respect of the franchisor, (i.e., obliging the subfranchisee to transfer to the franchisor the relevant assets upon termination of the subfranchise agreement), the franchisor must also be part of the relevant agreement.

The parties must determine whether such provisions must be included in the agreement and, if so, the mechanism to calculate the value of these assets.

VII. Termination

Please advise us as to any laws relating to termination in your country, such as agency laws, required indemnity provisions, notice or "good cause" requirements, or other laws affecting termination of a franchise agreement. Please describe.

As mentioned above in Section I, in the absence of a specific regime governing the franchise agreement, the Civil Code rules apply. Causes for termination are those which are commonly accepted, such as (i) mutual agreement, (ii) unilateral termination, and (iii) the occurrence of any of the events as may be agreed between the parties. In the event of termination by one of the parties, compensation for damages must be paid.

VIII. Governing Law, Jurisdiction, and Dispute Resolution

A. Choice of Law of Foreign Jurisdiction

Please confirm whether the choice of law of a foreign jurisdiction would likely to be upheld under the law of the country, except for certain matters such as trademarks, bankruptcy, and competition matters, which we assume would be governed by the law in your country.

The Civil Code sets out the general principle that the parties may freely choose the law governing their agreements provided that such choice of law corresponds to a serious interest of the parties and has a relevant connection with an element of the contract. A foreign law is deemed to have a connection with the underlying contract if it is the law of: (i) the domicile of the parties (or of one of them); (ii) the place of performance of the contractual obligations (place of shipment of the goods or acceptance of orders, place of payment, etc.); or (iii) the place where the contract was executed.

In the absence of such a relevant connection, the other party may claim that the choice of law and the election of a certain court does not serve any serious legally protected interest and the Cape Verdean courts may consider themselves as having competence to rule on the case.

The abovementioned choice of law principle is limited by the conflict of laws principles included in Cape Verdean law. In accordance with such principles, the law of a foreign jurisdiction shall not be applicable if deemed contrary to (i) the public policy principles of Cape Verdean Law (which will always apply, even if the governing law chosen by the parties is not Cape Verdean law), and to (ii) the mandatory provisions of Cape Verdean law. A provision qualifies as mandatory whenever the law expressly states so.

In the absence of a treaty or convention between Cape Verde and the relevant country on the recognition and enforcement of foreign awards, a judgment passed by a foreign court would have to be confirmed by the Cape Verdean Supreme Court[3] to be enforceable in Cape Verde. This confirmation process is purely formal and the Supreme Court limits its intervention to the verification of the compliance with the principles of due process of law and little more to issue the "exequatur" and allow the enforcements of the judgment before the lower courts (no decision on the merits involved).

---

[3] Pursuant to the Cape Verdean Civil Procedure Code, the Courts of Appeals are the courts with jurisdiction to entertain procedures for the recognition and confirmation of foreign decisions. The Courts of Appeals, however, have not yet been installed, therefore according to *Law 88/VII/2011, February 14, 2011 on the organization, operation and jurisdiction of the law courts*, the Supreme Court shall remain the court with jurisdiction for such procedures until they come into operation for the Courts of Appeals.

Cape Verde

B. International Arbitration Dispute Resolution

Please confirm that a court in your country would honor an election of international arbitration dispute resolution, and therefore refuse to hear any disputes arising under a franchise agreement.

As to the choice of a foreign venue for any arbitral proceedings, *Cape Verdean Arbitration Law* (*Law 76/VI/2005, of August 16, 2005*) recognizes the concept of "international arbitration" and allows the parties to choose the venue at which the arbitral proceedings are to take place.

Cape Verde is not a signatory of the *Convention on the Recognition and Enforcement of Foreign Arbitral Awards* (the "New York Convention"). This does not, however, mean that Cape Verde will not recognize and enforce foreign arbitral awards.

In accordance with the Cape Verdean Civil Procedure Code, (approved by *Legislative Decree 7/2010, July 1, 2010*, and rectified on September 27, 2010) and the Arbitration Law, to be enforceable in Cape Verde foreign arbitral awards are subject to recognition and confirmation by the Supreme Court. This procedure consists of a formal review of the relevant foreign arbitral award and does not imply a rehearing or any other decision on the merits of the case.

Foreign arbitral awards will be recognized and enforced in Cape Verde, unless:

- the arbitration agreement is not valid under the governing law thereof;

- the party against which the enforcement is sought was not given proper notice of the appointment of the arbitrator or of the arbitration proceedings, or its procedural rights was otherwise denied;

- the award concerns a dispute not comprised in the arbitration clause, or contains matters beyond the scope of the arbitration. In such case the award may only be enforced to the extent that it contains decisions on matters validly submitted to arbitration;
- the constitution of the arbitral court or the arbitral was not in accordance with agreement of the parties or, failing such agreement, with the law of the place where the hearing took place (the "lex loci arbitri");
- the award has not yet become enforceable upon the parties, or has been set aside or suspended by a court of competent court, either in the country where the award was issued or pursuant to the law of the arbitration agreement;
- the matter under dispute could not be referred to arbitration;
- the recognition or the enforcement of the awards would contravene Cape Verdean public order; or
- the country where the award was issued would not recognize or enforce an arbitral award issued in Cape Verde.

IX. Non-Competition Provisions

If the franchise agreement prohibits the master franchisee from engaging in certain competitive activities during the term of the agreement, and for a 12-month period after the termination or expiration of the agreement, please comment on the enforceability of non-competition covenants in your country.

It is common practice to include non-competition provisions in commercial agreements. Therefore, the parties in a franchise agreement may freely agree on non-competition provisions, such as the prohibition of the franchisee from engaging in certain competitive activities during the term of the agreement and for a 12-month period after the termination or expiration of the agreement, and such agreed rules would be considered enforceable.

In any case, it is common to extend the prohibition of competition (i) to affiliates and related persons/entities of the franchisee and (ii) for a certain period after termination of the franchise agreement. However, as previously noted, as a non-regulated agreement, the parties are free to agree on the existence of a non-competition provision and its terms, always in compliance with the general principles of the law.

X. Language Requirements

Does the law in your country require that a franchise agreement be translated into the local language in order to be enforceable between the parties?

The civil law allows private agreements to be executed in a foreign language. However, if an agreement is to be filed with any public authority in a foreign language, a Portuguese sworn translation is required.

By way of *Decree 1/2009, January 19, 2009*, the Cape Verdean government approved *The Hague Convention of October 5, 1961* ("Convention"), which waives the requirement of legalizing public documents from countries that are signatories to the Convention. The Convention entered into force in Cape Verde on February 10, 2010.

For the purposes of the Convention, public documents include (i) documents originated from an authority or official of a state, including the attorney general and the courts; (ii) administrative documents; (iii) acts carried out before or by a public notary; and (iv) official certificates that are placed on documents signed by persons in their private capacity, such as authentication of signatures by a notary.

Cape Verde

XI. Other Significant Matters

Please advise as to whether there are any significant matters not addressed above of which a franchisor should be aware in connection with its entering into a franchise agreement in your country.

There are no other significant matters to be addressed.

Cape Verde

Bibliography of International Franchise Resources

Kendal H. Tyre, Jr., Diana Vilmenay-Hammond, Pierce Haesung Han, Courtney L. Lindsay, II and Keri McWilliams

Nixon Peabody LLP

Washington, D.C.

I. General International Resources

Mark Abell, Gary R. Duvall, and Andrea Oricchio Kirsh, *International Franchise Legislation* B1, ABA FORUM ON FRANCHISING (1996)

Kathleen C. Anderson and Anthony M. Stiegler, *Put Muscle in Your Marks: Enforcing Intellectual Property Rights* W14, ABA FORUM ON FRANCHISING (1995)

Richard M. Asbill and Jane W. LaFranchi, *International Franchise Sales Laws—A Survey* W7, ABA FORUM ON FRANCHISING (2005)

Jeffery A. Brimer, Alison C. McElroy, and John Pratt, *Going International: What Additional Restraints Will You Face?* W4, ABA FORUM ON FRANCHISING (2011)

Michael G. Brennan, Alexander Konigsberg, and Philip F. Zeidman, *Globetrotting: A Workshop on International Franchising* 10/W8, ABA FORUM ON FRANCHISING (1994)

Michael G. Brennan, Alexander Konigsberg, and Philip F. Zeidman, *Globetrotting: Strategies for Launching U.S. Franchisors Abroad* 2/P2, ABA FORUM ON FRANCHISING (1994)

Christopher P. Bussert and Jennifer Dolman, *Regaining Your Trademark After Abandonment or Misappropriation* W7, ABA FORUM ON FRANCHISING (2011)

Ronald T. Coleman and Linda K. Stevens, *Trade Secrets and Confidential Information: Rights and Remedies* W2, ABA FORUM ON FRANCHISING (2000)

Finola Cunningham, *Commerce Department Helps Franchisors Go Global*, in FRANCHISING WORLD 63 (Dec. 2005)

Michael R. Daigle and Alex S. Konigsberg, *Meeting Off-Shore Disclosure and Contract Requirements* F/W13, ABA FORUM ON FRANCHISING (1992)

Jennifer Dolman, Robert A. Lauer, and Lawrence M. Weinberg, *Structuring International Master Franchise Relationships for Success and Responding When Things Go Awry* W22, ABA FORUM ON FRANCHISING (2007)

Gary R. Duvall, Paul Jones, and Jane LaFranchi, *Planning for the International Enforcement of Franchise Agreements* W6, ABA FORUM ON FRANCHISING (1999)

William Edwards, *International Expansion: Do Opportunities Outweigh Challenges?* in FRANCHISING WORLD (February 2008)

George J. Eydt and Stuart Hershman, *Bringing a Foreign Franchise System to the United States* W9, ABA FORUM ON FRANCHISING (2009)

William A. Finkelstein and Louis T. Pirkey, *International Trademarks* W15, ABA FORUM ON FRANCHISING (1991)

William A. Finkelstein, *Protecting Trademarks Internationally: Current Strategies and Developments* B3, ABA FORUM ON FRANCHISING (1996)

Stephen Giles, Lou H. Jones, and Lawrence Weinberg, *Negotiating and Documenting Complex International Franchise Agreements* W21, ABA FORUM ON FRANCHISING (2006)

Steven M. Goldman, Stephen Giles, Marc Israel, and Stanley Wong, *Competition Round Up from Around the World* LB2, ABA FORUM ON FRANCHISING (2004)

David C. Gryce and E. Lynn Perry, *Trademarks and Copyrights in the International Arena* 6/W4, ABA FORUM ON FRANCHISING (1993)

Kenneth S. Kaplan, Andrew P. Loewinger, and Penelope J. Ward, *System Standards in International Franchising* W14, ABA FORUM ON FRANCHISING (2005)

Edward Levitt and Jorge Mondragon, *A Survey of International Legal Traps and How to Avoid Them—Beyond the Franchise Laws* W20, ABA FORUM ON FRANCHISING (2007)

Ned Levitt, Kendal H. Tyre, and Penny Ward, *The Impossible Dream: Controlling Your International Franchise System* W4, ABA FORUM ON FRANCHISING (2010)

Michael K. Lindsey and Andrew P. Loewinger, *International (Non-U.S.) Franchise Disclosure Requirements* W9, ABA FORUM ON FRANCHISING (2002)

Andrew P. Loewinger and John Pratt, *Recent Changes and Trends in International Franchise Laws* W4, ABA FORUM ON FRANCHISING (2008)

Andrew P. Loewinger and Thomas M. Pitegoff, *Avoiding the Long Arm of the Law in International Franchising: Issues and Approaches* W8, ABA FORUM ON FRANCHISING (1995)

Craig J. Madson and Katherine C. Spelman, *Similarity and Confusion in the Intellectual Property Arena* W11, ABA FORUM ON FRANCHISING (1997)

Christopher A. Nowak, John Pratt, and Carl E. Zwisler, *Franchising Internationally with Countries with Opaque Legal Systems* W20, ABA FORUM ON FRANCHISING (2006)

E. Lynn Perry and John L. Sullivan Jr., *Trademark Compliance and Enforcement Techniques* E/W12, ABA FORUM ON FRANCHISING (1992)

Marcel Portmann, *Franchising Sector Proves Global Reach,* in FRANCHISING WORLD (January 2007)

John Pratt and Luiz Henrique O. do Amaral, *Civil Law for Common Law Practitioners (or How to Draft an Agreement for Use Overseas)* W4, ABA FORUM ON FRANCHISING (2002)

Kirk W. Reilly, Robert F. Salkowski and Geoffrey B. Shaw, *Determining the Rules of Engagement in Litigation Here and Abroad* W5, ABA FORUM ON FRANCHISING (2008)

Catherine Riesterer and Frank Zaid, *Basics of International Franchising* L/B2, ABA FORUM ON FRANCHISING (1997)

W. Andrew Scott and Christopher N. Wormald, *Stranger in a Strange Land: Contrasting Franchising in International Expansion* W2, ABA FORUM ON FRANCHISING (2003)

Donald Smith and Erik Wulff, *International Franchising: The Unraveling of an International Franchise Relationship* 15/W13, ABA FORUM ON FRANCHISING (1993)

Frank Zaid, Pamela Mills, and Michael Santa Maria, *Essential Issues in International Franchising* LB/1, ABA FORUM ON FRANCHISING (2001)

II. African Resources

Joyce G. Mazero and J. Perry Maisonneuve, *Franchising in the Middle East and North Africa* W2, ABA FORUM ON FRANCHISING (2009)

Kendal H. Tyre, Jr. and Diana Vilmenay-Hammond, *Franchise World: A Burgeoning Middle Class Spurs Franchise Investment in Africa*, MINORITY BUSINESS ENTREPRENEUR (November 2012)

Kendal H. Tyre, Jr., *IP Protection May Promote Additional Franchise Growth in Africa*, NIXON PEABODY LLP: FRANCHISING BUSINESS & LAW ALERT (September 2012)

Kendal H. Tyre, Jr., *Market Potential for Franchising in Africa*, NIXON PEABODY LLP: FRANCHISING BUSINESS & LAW ALERT (June 2011)

Kendal H. Tyre, Jr. and Courtney L. Lindsay, II, *Continued Growth of Franchising in Africa*, NIXON PEABODY LLP: FRANCHISE LAW ALERT (April 2013)

Kendal H. Tyre, Jr. and Courtney L. Lindsay, II, *Pan African Franchise Federation Holds Inaugural Meeting*, NIXON PEABODY LLP: AFRICA ALERT (June 2013)

Kendal H. Tyre, Jr. and Courtney L. Lindsay, II, *White House Encouraging Private Investment and Transparency in Sub-Saharan Africa*, NIXON PEABODY LLP: AFRICA ALERT (August 2012)

Kendal H. Tyre, Jr. and Diana Vilmenay-Hammond, *African Economic Growth Impacts Franchising on the Continent*, NIXON PEABODY LLP: FRANCHISE LAW ALERT (July 2012)

Kendal H. Tyre, Jr. and Diana Vilmenay-Hammond, *Franchising in Africa*, in FRANCHISING WORLD (August 2013)

John Sotos and Sam Hall, *African Franchising: Cross-Continent Momentum*, in FRANCHISING WORLD (June 2007)

A. Angola

João Afonso Fialho, *Franchising in Angola*, in FRANCHISING IN AFRICA: LEGAL AND BUSINESS CONSIDERATIONS 91-105 (Kendal H. Tyre, Jr. & Diana Vilmenay-Hammond eds. 2012)

B. Botswana

Bonzo Makgalemele, *Franchising in Botswana*, in FRANCHISING IN AFRICA: LEGAL AND BUSINESS CONSIDERATIONS 107-117 (Kendal H. Tyre, Jr. & Diana Vilmenay-Hammond eds. 2012)

C. Cape Verde

João Afonso Fialho, *Franchising in Cape Verde*, in FRANCHISING IN AFRICA: LEGAL AND BUSINESS CONSIDERATIONS 119-132 (Kendal H. Tyre, Jr. & Diana Vilmenay-Hammond eds. 2012)

D. Egypt

Girgis Abd El-Shahid, *Franchising in Eqypt*, in FRANCHISING IN AFRICA: LEGAL AND BUSINESS CONSIDERATIONS 133-142 (Kendal H. Tyre, Jr. & Diana Vilmenay-Hammond eds. 2012)

A. Safaa El Din El Oteifi, *Egypt*, in INTERNATIONAL FRANCHISING EGY/1 (Dennis Campbell gen. ed. 2011)

E. Ethiopia

Yohannes Assefa and Biset Beyene Molla, *Franchising in Ethiopia*, in FRANCHISING IN AFRICA: LEGAL AND BUSINESS CONSIDERATIONS 143-157 (Kendal H. Tyre, Jr. & Diana Vilmenay-Hammond eds. 2012)

Kendal H. Tyre, Jr., Yohannes Assefa and Getachew Mengistie Alemu, *New Intellectual Property Regulation Requires Scramble to Protect Marks in Ethiopia*, NIXON PEABODY LLP: AFRICA ALERT (October 2013)

F. Ghana

Divine K.D. Letsa and Hawa Tejansie Ajei, *Franchising in Ghana*, in FRANCHISING IN AFRICA: LEGAL AND BUSINESS CONSIDERATIONS 159-167 (Kendal H. Tyre, Jr. & Diana Vilmenay-Hammond eds. 2012)

G. Libya

Kendal H. Tyre, Jr. & Diana Vilmenay-Hammond, *First U.S. Franchise Opens in Libya*, NIXON PEABODY LLP: AFRICA ALERT (August 2012)

H. Mozambique

Diogo Xavier da Cunha, *Franchising in Mozambique*, in FRANCHISING IN AFRICA: LEGAL AND BUSINESS CONSIDERATIONS 169-182 (Kendal H. Tyre, Jr. & Diana Vilmenay-Hammond eds. 2012)

I. Nigeria

Theo Emuwa and Bimbola Fowler-Ekar, *Franchising in Nigeria*, in FRANCHISING IN AFRICA: LEGAL AND BUSINESS CONSIDERATIONS 183-198 (Kendal H. Tyre, Jr. & Diana Vilmenay-Hammond eds. 2012)

Kendal H. Tyre, Jr. and Theo Emuwa, *Nigerian Franchising: Making Your Way Through the Thicket*, NIXON PEABODY LLP: FRANCHISE LAW ALERT (June 2005)

J. South Africa

Eugene Honey, *Franchising and the New Consumer Protection Bill*, BOWMAN GILFILLAN (March 2008)

Eugene Honey, *Franchising and the Consumer Protection Bill*, BOWMAN GILFILLAN (May 2008)

Eugene Honey, *Pitfalls and Difficulties with the CPA*, ADAMS & ADAMS (March 2013)

Eugene Honey, *Disclosure is Compulsory*, ADAMS & ADAMS (May 2013)

Eugene Honey and Wim Alberts, *Fundamental Consumer Rights: The Right to Equality*, BOWMAN GILFILLAN (March 2009)

Eugene Honey and Wim Alberts, *The Reach of the Consumer Protection Bill: The Final*, BOWMAN GILFILLAN (March 2009)

Eugene Honey, *South Africa*, in GETTING THE DEAL THROUGH: FRANCHISE (2013) 172-178 (Philip F. Zeidman ed. 2013)

Taswell Papier, *Franchising in South Africa*, in FRANCHISING IN AFRICA: LEGAL AND BUSINESS CONSIDERATIONS 199-224 (Kendal H. Tyre, Jr. & Diana Vilmenay-Hammond eds. 2012)

Kendal H. Tyre, Jr., *A New Legal Landscape for Franchising in South Africa*, NIXON PEABODY LLP: FRANCHISING BUSINESS & LAW ALERT (September 2009)

K. Tunisia

Yessine Ferah, *Franchising in Tunisia*, in FRANCHISING IN AFRICA: LEGAL AND BUSINESS CONSIDERATIONS 225-245 (Kendal H. Tyre, Jr. & Diana Vilmenay-Hammond eds. 2012)

Kendal H. Tyre, Jr., Diana Vilmenay-Hammond, and Yessine Ferah, *New Franchise Legislation in Tunisia*, NIXON PEABODY LLP: FRANCHISE LAW ALERT (September 2010)

L. Zambia

Mabvuto Sakala, *Franchising in Zambia*, in FRANCHISING IN AFRICA: LEGAL AND BUSINESS CONSIDERATIONS 247-255 (Kendal H. Tyre, Jr. & Diana Vilmenay-Hammond eds. 2012)

14722467.1

Printed in Dunstable, United Kingdom

91343670R00030